SCIENCE FACT

SHAPES & STRUCTURES

JON RICHARDS

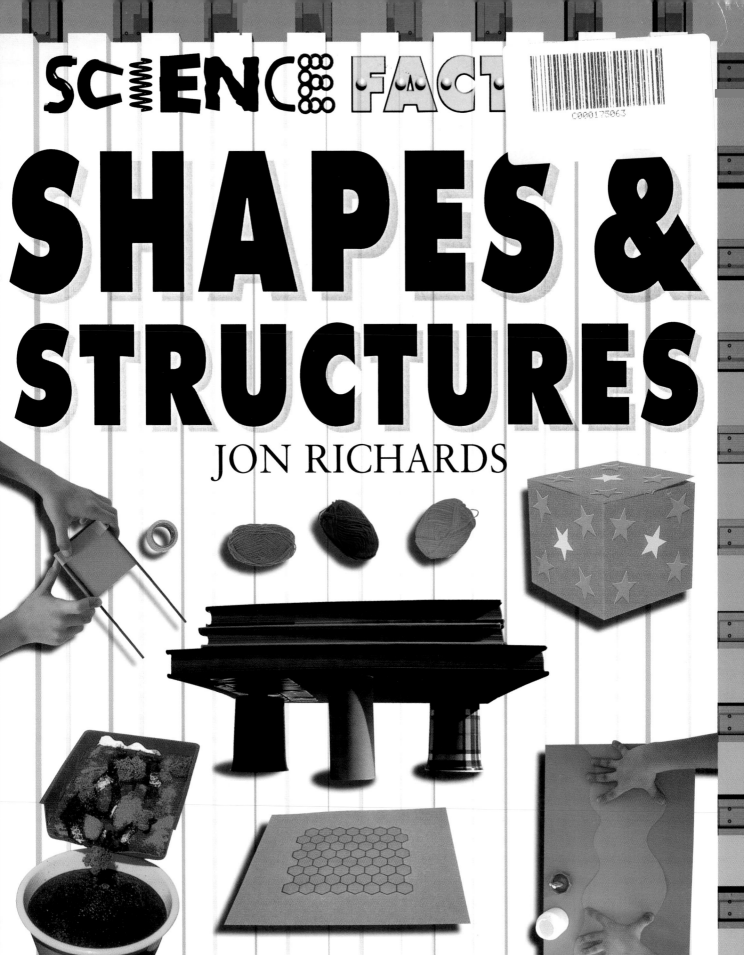

FRANKLIN WATTS
LONDON • SYDNEY

© Aladdin Books Ltd 2000

Designed and produced by
Aladdin Books Ltd
28 Percy Street
London W1P 0LD

ISBN 0 7496 3436 7 (hardcover)
ISBN 0 7496 4726 4 (paperback)

First published in Great Britain
in 2000 by
Franklin Watts Books
96 Leonard Street
London EC2A 4XD

Editor
Kathy Gemmell

Design

David West
Children's Book Design

Designer
Jennifer Skelly

Illustrator
Ian Moores

Printed in the U.A.E.

The author, Jon Richards, has written
a number of science and technology
books for children.

The consultant, Steve Parker, has
worked on over 150 books for
children, mainly on a science theme.

All the photos in this book were
taken by Roger Vlitos.

INTRODUCTION

Every object, large or small, has
a shape and a structure. Some
shapes fit together better than
others, and some materials are
stronger than others. Read on
and discover the properties of
different materials. Find out
which shapes and which
materials are best for building
strong structures, such as
skyscrapers and bridges.

CONTENTS

YOUR FACTORY

BEFORE YOU START any of the projects, it is important that you learn a few simple rules about the care of your science factory.

● Always keep your hands and the work surfaces clean. Dirt can damage results and ruin a project.

● Read the instructions carefully before you start each project.

● Make sure you have all the equipment you need for the project (see checklist opposite).

● If you haven't got the right piece of equipment, then improvise. For example, any paper that you can see through will do just as well as tracing paper.

● Don't be afraid to make mistakes. Just start again – patience is very important.

Equipment checklist:
- Cocktail sticks
- Paints and powder paint
- Large bowl, saucepan and jug
- Scissors, sticky tape and glue
- Metal and plastic lids, marbles
- Wooden disc and wooden blocks
- Sand and soil
- Plaster of Paris, modelling clay and model trees
- Bottle top, washing-up liquid and a watch
- Plastic bag, sheet of plastic, plastic tray and plastic cups
- String, ruler, pens, coloured pencils, coins and books
- Paper, thick card, coloured card and tissue paper
- Cardboard boxes, cardboard and thick cardboard tubes
- Table-tennis ball, empty spray can and wooden spoon
- Cloth, tracing paper, wooden dowels
- Stiff wire and a saw
- Coloured wool and pipe cleaners
- Milk, vinegar and lard
- Hexagon stencil and a weight

WARNING:
Some of the projects in this book need the help of an adult. Always ask a grown-up to give you a hand with sharp objects such as scissors.

HANDLING HEAT

IN DECIDING WHICH MATERIALS to use when making something, designers and engineers must decide which materials are best suited to a particular job. For example, it would be no good making a saucepan out of plastic because it would melt as soon as you put it on the stove. Sometimes they may even need to test various materials to find out which works best for the task. This project lets you test several materials to find out which is the best at conducting heat.

FEEL THE HEAT

1 *Cut out three pieces of paper the same size. Tape each piece of paper to a cocktail stick to make three flags. Decorate each flag differently using the coloured pencils.*

KEEPING IT HOT

Collect cups made from different materials, such as metal, plastic and china. Fill them with the same amount of hot water. Leave for several minutes. Then, using a thermometer, find out which cup is the best at keeping the water hot.

2 *Cut three lumps of lard which are the same size. Place one lump of lard on each of the metal and plastic lids and the wooden disc. Push a flag into each lump of lard.*

WHY IT WORKS

3 Ask an adult to fill a large bowl with hot water. Place the lids and the disc in the bowl so that they float.

The flag on the metal lid drops first because the tiny molecules which make up the lid conduct heat very well (1). Heat energy from the water passes quickly from one molecule to the next, until it reaches the lard, causing it to melt. The flag on the wooden disc (2) will be the last to drop because wood molecules are bad heat conductors.

(2)

(1)

4 Using a watch, time how long it takes for each piece of lard to melt and each flag to drop. Which of the three flags drops first and which drops last?

TESTING MATERIALS

WHAT YOU NEED
Paper
Tissue paper
Plastic bag
Sticky tape
Wooden dowels
Three plastic cups
String, Scissors
Marbles
Coloured card

THE LAST PROJECT SHOWED how to test materials to see which was the best conductor of heat. Another important property of a material is its strength. A material must be strong enough for the job it has to do – one that breaks under the slightest pressure may be dangerous if used for the wrong thing. This project shows how to find which of three materials can carry the heaviest load.

WHY IT WORKS

The plastic bag strip can carry the most weight because the tiny molecules which make up the plastic are held together by very strong bonds. The tissue paper is the weakest strip because it is made up of fibres which are not very densely packed and come apart easily.

TISSUE PAPER   PLASTIC   PAPER

CARRYING THE LOAD

1 Cut three strips – from the paper, tissue paper and the plastic bag. Make sure that they are all the same width.

2 Tape one wooden dowel to the top and bottom of each strip.

3 Cut some string and tie it in a big loop. Cross the middle of the loop over the bottom of each of the plastic cups and tape it in place, as shown.

4 Loop a cup over one of the dowels on each strip, as shown. Tie another string loop to the dowel at the other end of each strip.

STRIP TESTING

Repeat the test with three strips of the same plastic, each of a different width. Which carries most weight?

5 Make a stand from coloured card and push three dowels through it, as shown. Hang the strips from the dowels. Add marbles to the cups until the strips break. Which one breaks first?

9

SPRINGY MATERIALS

YOU MIGHT HAVE NOTICED that some materials, no matter how much you stretch, crush, bend or twist them, will always go back to their original shape and size. Sometimes it is important to use flexible materials like this. For example, a plane's wings are designed to bend a little to absorb the force exerted on them by flying. This project lets you have fun with a material's flexibility.

JACK-IN-THE-BOX

1 *Make a spring by coiling stiff wire around an empty spray can.*

2 *Paint a face on the table-tennis ball. Tape a pipe cleaner to the bottom of the ball for your jack's body. Make a hat from some cloth.*

3 *Tape the bottom of the pipe cleaner body to a bottle top. Tightly wind one end of the spring around the bottle top. Use pipe cleaners to make arms. Make clothes and gloves from the cloth.*

4 *Decorate the cardboard box using the paints.*

5 *Tape a short piece of thick cardboard tube to the bottom of the box. Make sure the spring fits snugly inside the tube.*

WHY IT WORKS

Most materials have elasticity – they can resume their shape after being squashed. In a spring at rest (1), all the forces acting on it are balanced. Squeezing increases the forces that make the spring want to spring apart (2). Releasing the spring causes it to push apart again.

(1)

(2)

HANGING DOWN

Fix a weight to the end of a ruler. Hang it over the edge of a table. Now move the ruler so it hangs further over the edge. Does it bend more?

6 Put the spring inside the tube, then push the jack down into the box and close the lid. Open the lid quickly and watch the jack spring up out of the box.

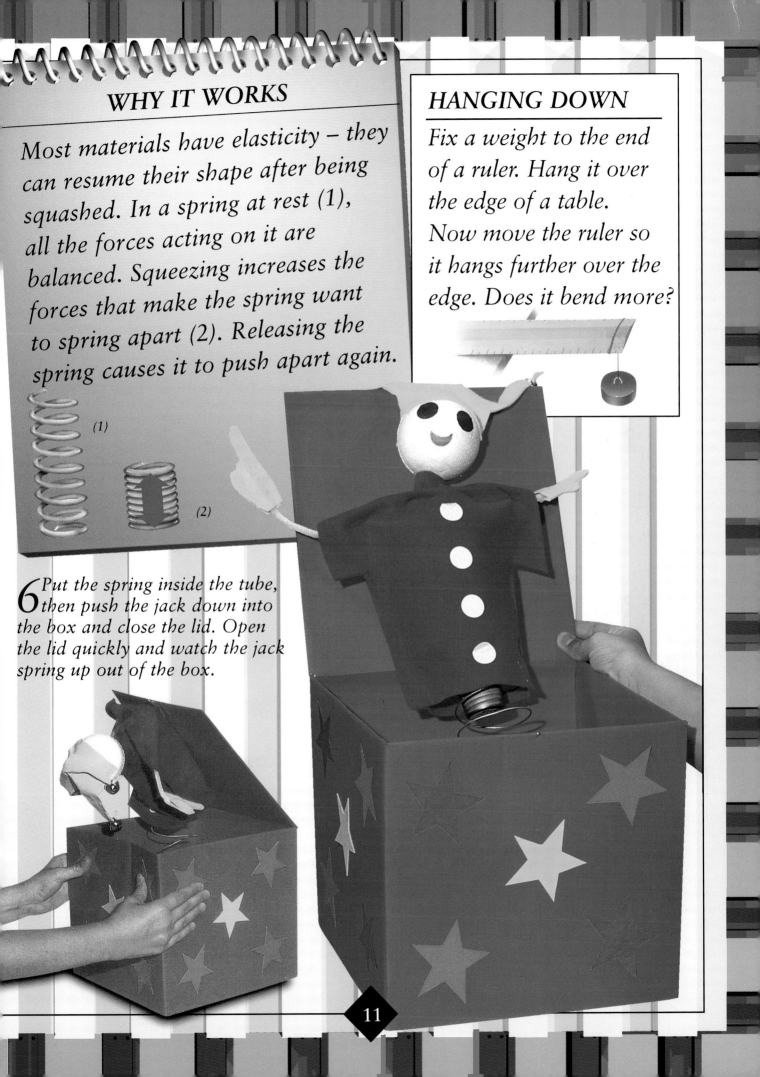

MAKING PLASTICS

WHAT YOU NEED
Milk
Saucepan
Vinegar
Paints
Wooden spoon

THE LAST PROJECT SHOWED you how to make metal wire elastic by coiling it into a spring. But some substances do not return to their original shape when pulled out of it. These are plastic substances. Wet clay is plastic because you can mould it into any shape and it stays that way. This project shows how you can turn everyday ingredients into a plastic material.

PLASTIC POT

Place a plastic yoghurt pot in a saucepan. Ask an adult to pour boiling water over it. Watch as it loses its shape.

PLASTIC MILK

1 *Ask an adult to slowly warm some milk in a saucepan.*

2 *Just as the milk is starting to bubble, slowly stir in some vinegar.*

WHY IT WORKS

When the vinegar is added to the milk, it starts a chemical reaction. This causes the tiny molecules that make up the milk to clump together. Instead of being runny and free to move, as they are in the liquid milk, the molecules form one large lump. This lump is your plastic material.

MILK MOLECULES
CLUMP TOGETHER

3 Keep stirring and adding vinegar. Within a few seconds the mixture should turn rubbery.

6 Decorate your plastic with paints.

4 Once it has turned rubbery, let the mixture cool. Ask an adult to put it in the sink.

5 Ask an adult to put some of the cooled mixture on a plate. Run it under cold water until it is completely cold.

SHAPING MATERIALS

PLASTIC MATERIALS CAN CHANGE SHAPE without returning to their original structure, as you saw when you made a plastic substance in the last project. Plaster of Paris is a substance that can take on the shape of any container or mould it is poured into. It starts as a powder-like substance that can be mixed with water to form a paste. The paste then sets hard. This project shows you how to mould plaster of Paris.

WHAT YOU NEED
Thick card
Sticky tape
Scissors
Modelling clay
Washing-up liquid
Plaster of Paris

MOULDING SHAPES

1 *Ask an adult to make a frame out of thick card. Tape it to another piece of card, as shown here. Make a pattern out of modelling clay in the base of your frame.*

2 *Cover the modelling clay shape with washing-up liquid. This will stop the plaster of Paris from sticking to the modelling clay.*

3 *Mix the plaster of Paris with some water and pour this into the mould.*

4 *Cover the modelling clay completely and leave the plaster to harden.*

14

WHY IT WORKS

When plaster of Paris is mixed with water, it forms a paste which can be poured into a mould. Over time, the water evaporates (goes off into the air as a gas) and the paste hardens to form a brittle substance.

PLASTER OF PARIS

WATER

PLASTER PICTURES

Use your mould to make shapes from modelling clay. Simply press the clay into the plaster and it will take on the pattern of the mould.

5 When the plaster is dry, gently remove it from the frame. You will see that the plaster has hardened with the shape of the modelling clay set into it.

WEAVING MATERIALS

SOME MATERIALS ARE ONLY strong in one direction and are not good on their own for using in structures. One way around this weakness is to weave strands of material together. This creates a new structure which uses its strengths in all directions. Clothing fibres are an example of this. They combine threads to create usable materials. Learn how to weave strands of wool in this project.

WHY IT WORKS

The strings running up and down your loom are called warp threads. The wool strands which you weave across the loom are called weft threads. By weaving the threads together, the finished fabric is strong. The closer the weave, the stronger the fabric.

WEFT THREAD

WARP THREAD

SMOOTH FIBRES

Have a look at the ends of different threads of material with a magnifying glass. Compare the sizes of each fibre and see how smooth the ends are.

MAKE A LOOM

1 To make your loom, ask an adult to cut an odd number of notches along the top and bottom of a piece of thick card.

2 Wind a length of string around each pair of notches and knot each loop at the back of your loom.

3 Weave a strand of wool in and out of each length of string. Make sure you push each row up into the one above it. To change colour, tie your new wool onto the end of the old strand.

4 When you have finished, knot the last piece of wool and lift the fabric off your loom. Push two wooden dowels through the top and bottom of your material and hang it up as a decoration.

GETTING STRONGER

SOMETIMES ONE MATERIAL ON ITS OWN is not suitable for a job, and two or more different materials may need to be combined to create the right material. Fibreglass, for example, contains tiny pieces of glass in a plastic, which makes it both flexible and strong. In this project, see how you can strengthen plaster of Paris by adding another material.

WHY IT WORKS

The block of plaster alone (1) is brittle and will break when a strong force is applied to it. The block that contains the metal wire (2) will last longer because it can bend a little and absorb the knocks it receives.

(1)   (2)

REINFORCED PLASTER

1 Use the frame you made and follow the steps on page 14 to make one block of plaster of Paris. (You don't need to make the mould.)

2 When the block is dry, remove it from the frame. You need to make another block the same size, but before you start, lay some pieces of wire into the frame.

CLAY BRICKS

Make bricks out of clay and leave them to harden. Now make more bricks of the same size, but this time mix some straw into the clay. Test them for strength and find out which ones last the longest.

5 *Swing the weight at the blocks of plaster. Make sure that you hit each block at the same spot and that you release the weight from the same distance each time.*

3 *Lay the wires both across and lengthways, as shown here. Now make your second block of plaster with the wires embedded in it.*

6 *You will find that the block with the metal wire will last a lot longer before it shatters than the block without any wire.*

4 *Ask an adult to cut out cardboard supports. Lean the blocks against these on a sheet of plastic, as shown. Tie a weight to a length of string. Tie up the string so that it can swing.*

NATURAL STRUCTURES

WHAT YOU NEED
Plastic tray
Large bowl
Jug of water
Modelling clay
Sand and soil
Green powder paint
Model trees
Saw

SOME OF THE LARGEST and most impressive structures found on this planet are not made by humans at all. Instead they have been formed naturally by the forces of the wind, sea, rivers or even by the movement of the massive plates of rock that make up the Earth's surface. These structures include soaring mountains, enormous canyons and towering waterfalls. This project shows you how a river can carve shapes and structures into the landscape.

FREEZING WATER

Water can change the shape of the land when it freezes. To see how, fill a plastic bottle with water. Screw the top on tightly. Put it in a sealed plastic bag in the freezer all night. The water expands as it freezes and shatters the plastic bottle.

7 *Slowly pour in water at the back of the tray. Watch it flow down the slope, carving a path into the sand and soil. Make sure you catch the water in a bowl.*

FLOWING RIVER

1 Ask an adult to saw off the front of a plastic tray.

2 Put some mounds of modelling clay around the bottom of the tray.

3 Pour the soil over the mounds so that they are covered. Make sure that the soil forms a slope from the back of the tray down to the open front.

4 Cover the soil with a layer of dry sand.

5 Now cover the sand with a layer of green powder paint to give a grass effect.

6 Add some model trees. Make a record of what it looks like by drawing or taking a photograph.

WHY IT WORKS

Water always flows down a slope (1). As it does so, it picks up soil particles and carries them along. The more soil it carries, the more it changes the landscape around it. Some rivers form huge bends called meanders (2). Over time, these bends are worn away, leaving small, crescent-shaped lakes called ox-bow lakes (3).

(3)

(2)

(1)

21

CHOOSING SHAPES

WHAT YOU NEED
Coloured card
Tracing paper
Scissors
Ruler
Pen
Hexagon stencil
Glue

OTHER PROJECTS IN THIS BOOK have shown you how to decide which material is the best for your structure. Another thing that designers and engineers have to decide is the shape of the structure. This project shows how shapes that fit together exactly are good for covering an area. They also make strong structures.

HEXAGON GAME

1 *Using a stencil, draw and cut out 64 hexagonal (six-sided) shapes from two colours of card. Make sure they are all the same size.*

2 *Now stencil onto a piece of card 64 hexagons which tessellate (fit together exactly). Trace the pattern and transfer it onto a sheet of coloured card.*

3 *Ask an adult to cut out both patterns and stick them together to make a strong grid. Go over the lines with a pen.*

4 *Stick your hexagon grid onto another, larger sheet of card.*

5 *Ask an adult to cut out this shape from card and fold it to make a small cube. Mark three sides with a 1 and the other three sides with a 2. This will be your game dice. Ask someone to play the hexagon game with you.*

MAKE A MOSAIC

Using lots of different shapes and colours, make a pattern or picture on card. This type of picture is called a mosaic.

Hexagons can cover the board because they tessellate. This means that they fit together exactly without overlapping or leaving gaps. Shapes that tessellate make strong structures. Bees use hexagons to make a honeycomb.

6 Take turns to roll the dice. The numbers will tell you how many hexagons you can put down. The aim is to get from one side of the board to the other.

TESTING SHAPES

YOU TESTED DIFFERENT TYPES of material for strength on pages 8-9. Strength is an important factor when deciding if the shape of a structure suits a task. Tessellating shapes are strong and are good for covering an area, as you saw in the last project. This project shows you how some shapes can be strong in one direction but very weak in another.

WHY IT WORKS

The shape of the tube means that it can take a lot of compressional (squeezing) force along its length. However, its sides are weak, and they will collapse when the slightest compressional force is applied there.

EGG STRENGTH

Repeat the project opposite, but this time use an egg instead of the tube. You will find that, like the tube, the egg can bear more weight when it is standing upright (you will need modelling clay to hold it in place) than when it is on its side.

1 Place a cardboard tube on its side. Stack coins on either side of the tube, until they are just below the width of the tube itself.

2 Start to balance books on top of the tube. Keep adding books until the tube collapses and the books rest on the stacks of coins.

3 Place the second tube on its end. Put plastic cups that are just smaller than the tube on either side.

4 Now repeat the project by placing books on top of the tube. See how many books have to be added before the tube collapses.

5 You will find that this time you need more books before the tube collapses.

TALL STRUCTURES

WHEN PUTTING TOGETHER A BUILDING, engineers and designers have to be aware of the stresses and forces that the building might be subjected to over its lifetime. They must then find the best materials and shapes to keep the building upright. This project shows you one solution for coping with the large forces a tall skyscraper has to put up with.

14cm

9cm

8cm

4cm

20cm

9cm

REACH FOR THE SKY

1 Ask an adult to cut out a number of rectangular shapes from the thick card, using the dimensions shown here. Cut slots in the longest pieces where the dotted lines are.

2 To form the basic unit of your skyscraper, put three of the longest pieces in a triangle and join them by pushing the smallest pieces into the slots, as shown. Glue on some coloured card for the windows.

3 Place the medium-sized pieces of card against the sides of the unit, as shown. Repeat step 2 to make lots of basic units.

The medium-sized and square pieces of card support the building by forming a broad base for each unit. This makes each level, and the structure as a whole, more stable. These triangular supporting structures are called buttresses.

BUTTRESS

CARD TOWER

Make a tower from playing cards. The triangular shape of each level is what makes the cards stable.

4 Cut out some squares of card measuring 9cm along the sides. To build your skyscraper, stack the basic units on top of each other. At each level, lean the card squares against the units, as shown.

5 See how high you can build your skyscraper.

27

BUILDING BRIDGES

WHAT YOU NEED
*Six wooden
blocks
Pencils
Sticky tape
Thick card
String, Glue
Coloured card
Modelling clay*

THE LAST PROJECT SHOWED you how to build upwards. But what happens if you have to build a structure that runs across something? Bridges give designers and engineers different problems. This project shows some of the ways that these problems can be overcome.

BRIDGING THE GAP

1 *Tape pencils to two corners of each wooden block, as shown here.*

2 *Ask an adult to cut out strips of thick card the same width as the wooden blocks. For the first bridge, simply place one strip between two of the blocks.*

3 *For the second bridge, tie string around two pencils, tape it to the middle of a card strip, as shown, then tie it to the pencils on another block.*

4 *For your third bridge, place another strip of card under the first strip and glue this to the wooden blocks and your bridge's roadway to form an arch.*

CANTILEVER BRIDGE

Another bridge structure is the cantilever bridge. Make your own cantilever bridge, as shown here, and see how much weight it can support.

WHY IT WORKS

Your first bridge will buckle quickly as it has no supporting structure for the road. The road held by the string, called a suspension bridge, will buckle next. The strongest bridge is the arch bridge. The arch shape is best at spreading any weight on the bridge over its whole length.

5 Make a river landscape with coloured card, as shown below. Fix the bridges to the landscape by pressing the pencils into modelling clay. Test the bridges by placing heavier and heavier weights on them. Find out which one can carry the most weight.

FINDING OUT MORE

ARCH This is a natural or artificial structure which crosses an open area in a curve. *Find out how an arch can make a bridge stronger in the project on pages 28-29.*

COMPRESSIONAL FORCE This is a force which squeezes something. *See how you can test different objects against compressional force in the project on pages 24-25.*

ELASTIC When a material is elastic, it is capable of returning to its original shape after it has been squashed or pulled. *You can find out how to make metal wire elastic in the project on pages 10-11.*

PLASTIC A material is plastic if it can be shaped when it is soft and then sets hard into its new shape. *See how to make plastic material on pages 12-13.*

STRONG SILK

Some of the silk that spiders make, which they use to spin their webs, is actually stronger than steel of the same thickness.

HOT STUFF

The tiles that cover the Space Shuttle are made from a material that can withstand the high temperatures of re-entering the Earth's atmosphere.

SKYSCRAPER This is a very tall building usually found in large cities. *Find out one way of keeping very tall buildings, such as skyscrapers, upright in the project on pages 26-27.*

INSIDE BONES

The bones in your body are not solid. Instead they are full of holes containing bone marrow and blood vessels. This means that they are strong as well as light.

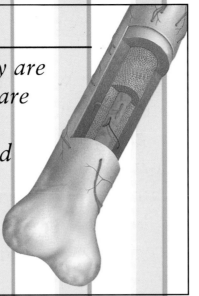

WARP THREADS

These are the threads that run up and down a material as it is being woven. You can learn how to weave your own material on pages 16-17.

SUSPENSION BRIDGE

This uses long cables hung from towers at either end of the bridge to help it take the weight of objects crossing it. Build your own suspension bridge in the project on pages 28-29.

TESSELLATE

When shapes tessellate, they cover an area completely without overlapping or leaving any gaps. Find out on pages 22-23 how you can use tessellating shapes to make a fun game to play.

WEFT THREADS

These are the threads that run across a material. See how weaving weft threads through warp threads on a loom can make a material in the project on pages 16-17.

CONCORDE

The windscreen of Concorde is covered in a very thin sheet of solid gold. This is because gold is very good at protecting the jetliner from the heat that is generated when it flies faster than the speed of sound.

INDEX

arch 29, 30

bridge 28, 29, 30, 31
buttress 27

cantilever bridge 28
chemical reaction 13
china 6
clay 12, 14, 15, 19, 21, 24, 29
compressional force 24, 30
conduction 6, 7, 8

elastic 11, 12, 30
energy 7
evaporation 15

fabric 16, 17
fibre 8, 16
fibreglass 18
flexibility 10, 18
force 10, 11, 18, 20, 24, 26, 30
freezing 20

glass 18

heat 6, 7, 8, 31
hexagon 22, 23

load 8
loom 16, 17, 31

material 6, 8, 10, 11, 13, 14, 16, 18, 22, 24, 26, 30, 31

meander 21
metal 6, 7, 19, 30
molecule 7, 8, 13
mosaic 23
mould 12, 14, 15

ox-bow lake 21

plaster of Paris 14, 15, 18, 19
plastic 6, 8, 9, 12, 13, 14, 18, 19, 20, 30
pressure 8

river 20, 21

skyscraper 26, 27, 30
spring 10, 11, 12
straw 19
strength 8, 16, 18, 19, 23, 24, 31
suspension bridge 29, 31

tessellation 22, 23, 24, 31

warp thread 16, 31

weft thread 16, 31

weight 8, 9, 11, 19, 28, 29, 31
wire 12, 18, 19